Chapter 1 · Prescription Miracles

Stephanie Dunn Haney would have been dead for eight years by now. In 2007, the thirty-nine-year-old nonsmoker and mother of two small girls was diagnosed with stage IV lung cancer. After her diagnosis, Stephanie was put on standard therapy for lung cancer: chemotherapy with Avastin, a drug designed to block blood supply to tumors. Her cancer initially responded to treatment but then grew resistant, as most cancers do.

So her doctors switched her to a targeted cancer medicine, which bought her more time. Her tumors again grew resistant to the new medicine, but by that time she qualified for a clinical trial to test a new drug. Researchers had recently discovered that a small percentage of lung cancer patients have a defective gene that promotes tumor growth, called ALK. The trial was testing a drug designed to block ALK expression, and Stephanie's tumor both contained the gene and responded to the experimental drug.

As of May 2016, Stephanie had been living with metastatic lung cancer for nine years. Yet, she described her life as "relatively normal." But in 2007, the ability to lead a "normal" existence wouldn't have been predicted. That year, Stephanie wrote she had "learned a majority of

late-stage lung cancer patients die within one year. Just one year. One birthday. One summer."

Now take the case of Emily Whitehead, who was just five years old when she was diagnosed with leukemia. After her cancer resisted standard treatments twice, her parents enrolled her in a clinical trial at the Children's Hospital of Philadelphia, where researchers extracted immune-system T cells from her body, genetically modified them to attack her cancerous B cells, and then reinjected them. Today, she is a happy, thriving ten-year-old – and has been cancer-free for the past four years.

Thanks to many advances in treatment and detection, stories like those of Stephanie and Emily are increasingly common. That means more birthdays, holidays, weddings, and anniversaries to celebrate. Cancer mortality has fallen by 23 percent over the past two decades.

More Americans than ever are living longer with a cancer diagnosis. Better drugs with fewer side effects also mean that many of those diagnosed with the disease can return to work and live relatively normal lives for longer periods of time. New treatments will eventually allow us to manage cancer in a similar way to how we do chronic illnesses like diabetes or HIV/AIDs. Customized cures targeted to the biology of individual patients like Stephanie are also being developed to enable greater success in the treatment of severe depression, heart disease, diabetes, and Parkinson's.

It's no exaggeration to say that America stands on the cusp of a Golden Age of Medicine. A look back at just the last few decades shows astonishing progress across many diseases. Patients with the blood-clotting disorder hemophilia used to have an average lifespan of just thirteen years. Today, thanks to effective blood-clotting treatments, people diagnosed with the disease decades ago are now planning for their lives after they retire in their midsixties.

Thanks to many advances in treatment and detection, stories like those of Stephanie and Emily are increasingly common. That means more birthdays, holidays, weddings, and anniversaries to celebrate.

New approaches like gene therapy may eventually allow these patients to wean themselves off of daily injections of clotting factor, a functional cure.

From 1969 to 2013, death rates from heart disease plummeted by 67 percent, thanks in part to lower smoking rates – but also thanks to the wider use of medicines like statins, which lower cholesterol. Since the 1970s, stroke-related mortality has fallen from third to fifth place as a leading cause of death in the United States. This is primarily due to the widespread use of effective drugs for hypertension.

New treatments for rheumatoid arthritis (RA) can slow or even halt this progressive joint disease that would have led to severe disability in the past. The last two decades have seen a 40 percent reduction in disability caused by RA, thanks to more aggressive treatment with effective medicines.

When the HIV/AIDS virus was first tentatively identified in the United States in 1983, after having incubated for decades in Africa, scientists were baffled and the public was terrified. There were predictions that AIDS would be the next "black death." But, by 1996, the FDA had approved the first combination HIV-AIDs drug cocktails, and they turned out to be life-saving treatments. Between 1996 and 1997, mortality rates fell by 40 percent. Today, many HIV-infected patients – especially when they are treated early on – can expect to have close-to-normal life spans.

Of course, not every treatment discovery will lead to similarly powerful breakthroughs, but even modest improvements delivered by a succession of new medicines can add up to large gains for patients facing serious chronic illnesses, which account for 86 percent of US health care spending.

Many diseases incubate in our bodies silently for decades before producing symptoms. The good news is that drug companies, medical researchers, and tech companies are joining forces to create and mine large databases containing genetic information and detailed patient histories to home in on the molecular drivers of complex chronic diseases. Over time, the new normal in medicine will become stopping diseases at their molecular inception – halting their progression before they become serious enough to generate clinical symptoms. A world with much-less disease-related suffering and death is the future our children and grandchildren will enjoy as a result.

The bad news is that it won't come fast enough to help many patients who need it today. And because many of these medicines are new, and are therefore still protected by patents and therefore expensive, they can come with high copays and coinsurance. For today's patient, the cost of hope can seem painfully high – if not out of reach. An August 2015 Kaiser Family Foundation poll found that 72 percent of Americans consider drug prices unreasonable, with 24 percent saying they're having difficulty affording the prescriptions. And 74 percent of respondents also think drug companies put profits before people.

If vulnerable patients are going without access to critical medicines because of high costs and copays, insurers, drug makers, and policy makers need to find solutions that broaden access.

And they need to start now.

But we need them to accomplish this without derailing the incentives driving the industry to innovate. Because America's laws allow for the market pricing of medicines, thus providing an incentive for private investors to finance the massive cost and long delays associated with drug innovation, we now lead the world in developing precision medicine for diseases once regarded as untreatable or incurable. The possibility of a big payday, should a new medicine be effective, is what keeps investors eagerly engaged in seeking the next breakthrough.

But who can blame Americans – suffering from stagnant wages and rising health care costs – for wanting the government to tamp down the cost of the prescription drugs they're paying more for at pharmacies and hospitals?

Again, there is good news and bad news. The good news is that there are things that Washington can do to allow prescription drug prices to fall naturally. The bad news is that none of these constructive solutions get enough attention in election years.

Instead, we mainly hear rhetoric that devalues and demonizes the drug industry. The Democratic presidential contender, Hillary Clinton, proudly calls the pharmaceutical industry one of her personal enemies. She wants the government to negotiate drug prices, and favors cheaper imports from Canada.

The Republican contender, Donald Trump, isn't much different. He has likened drug makers to public utilities, and promised to save $300 billion by having the government get tough when it buys drugs for Medicare.

Similar proposals are popping up outside Washington. In California, the AIDS Healthcare Foundation is sponsoring a ballot initiative that would prohibit state programs like Medi-Cal from purchasing any drug at a higher price than that paid by the Veteran's Administration. The VA commands steeper discounts, in part, as in-kind repayment for the military service of its patients.

In Massachusetts, the state attorney general threatened to sue the pharmaceutical company Gilead, jawboning the company to lower the price it charges the Bay State for its hepatitis-C drug, so that it comes closer to what the company charges poorer countries like India and Egypt.

But manufacturers must be assured that drugs are selling in richer countries like the United States before they'll sink money into drug development in the first place. Once they do, they can afford to sell at much-lower prices in poorer countries. Demanding Egyptian prices for the United States is a good way to get fewer drugs for wealthy Americans *and* fewer drugs for poor Egyptians.

Gilead's Sovaldi, approved by the FDA in late 2013 for the treatment of chronic hepatitis-C infection, was a giant leap forward in hepatitis treatment. Hep C is a disease that

Market competition also helps to keep drug prices in check – thanks in no small measure to powerful payers like Express Scripts and UnitedHealth that negotiate prices down.

kills more people in America than AIDS, and chronic HCV infection is the world's leading cause of liver cancer. Sovaldi offers about a 95 percent cure rate – better than the best previous treatment, Incivek, which was launched in 2011 by Gilead's competitor, Vertex. Incivik's cure rate being only 75 percent, its revenues plunged by 96 percent after Solvadi's launch, and Vertex withdrew the drug from the market.

What happened to Incivik as a result of the introduction of Sovaldi is the unappreciated norm in America's cutting-edge pharmaceutical market: competition. New and effective drugs can fail to catch on with doctors and patients, or fall out of favor because newer drugs render them obsolete overnight.

This is a risk that every innovating company, and its investors, must accept as a matter of course. The high list price of a drug when it's launched allows investors and innovators to be compensated for that uncertainty, and for generating the revenue necessary to fund ongoing research and development for the next generation of medicines.

Calling this industry "greedy" and advocating price controls (even de facto ones, like reducing the number of years a drug is patent protected to prevent generic competition) might win votes in the short run. But these policies undermine the incentives that encourage companies and their investors to make large, long-term investments in testing potential new medicines – the vast majority of which will turn out to be expensive failures. That lack of foresight – willful or not – can have deadly consequences for patients. If a drug doesn't exist, you can't argue about its price. Patients will languish and die without ever knowing what they've lost.

Is that really what we want?

Drug Prices and What You Pay: A Complex and Confusing Picture

Pharmaceuticals and biotech companies make up a rapidly evolving industry in which innovators race against the competition in an effort to bring better drugs to patients.

The necessity of these high-risk, high-reward investments for yielding the best-possible chance of developing cures for seriously ill patients is sometimes lost on the public, just as it was during the wave of outrage resulting from the announcement that Sovaldi's list price would be $84,000: $1,000 a day for twelve weeks of treatment.

Very few among us could afford to pay that out of pocket. And that's the whole point of insurance – to protect against the ruinously high costs of a serious illness or accident. A second role of insurers is to help keep prescription drug costs down by acting as a bulk purchaser of drugs for insured consumers . . . like a Costco for the pharmaceutical industry. Just as large national retailers can command deep discounts from manufacturers when it comes time to stock their many stores, insurers can play drug companies against one another to negotiate large rebates on medicines listed on their formularies.

As a result, most American consumers never pay the list price for a drug – but they also never know what the real rebate from the drug company to their insurer is. Deductibles, copays, coinsurance, and drug formularies can vary widely across health plans.

So while list prices grab the headlines, they often bear little resemblance to the actual prices paid by large private purchasers such as Express Scripts and UnitedHealth, or public programs like Medicaid (which enjoy deep discounts already mandated by law). In a 2016 op-ed for the *Wall Street Journal*, Eli Lilly CEO John Lechleiter pulled the curtain back on the mostly invisible discounts that manufacturers offer to payers. He wrote that the average discount to commercial payers is about 20 percent, while public program discounts can exceed 80 percent of a drug's list price.

Even when a drug's list price appears to rise quickly, drug company rebates are a big mitigating factor. A 2015 IMS Health study found that while list prices increased by over 14 percent in 2014, offsets from rebates resulted in the actual average increase only being 5 percent. That is about the same annual rate as general health care inflation, which drug prices tend to track.

Market competition also helps to keep drug prices in check – thanks in no small measure to powerful payers like Express Scripts and UnitedHealth that negotiate prices down. One large payer now claims that Sovaldi is even cheaper in the United States than in Europe, where price controls keep drug prices artificially low. How could that be true? Less than three years after Sovaldi's launch, several other highly effective drugs for hepatitis C that were in the pipeline have come to market. Jockeying for customers, drug companies have offered insurers rebates on new hep-C drugs that are as deep as 50 percent.

Discounts and rebates aside, high out-of-pocket costs for effective medicines are a problem that still needs solving. The Kaiser data also showed that out of the 54 percent of Americans who say they have taken a prescription drug recently, 72 percent think their medicines are easy to afford. That means about a quarter find it difficult to afford their prescription drugs. For lower-income Americans, and those suffering from chronic illness, even small copays can translate into big burdens.

But some critics of drug pricing appear to have trouble understanding that while there are workable solutions that can lower the cost of prescription drugs for patients, many short-term "solutions," like price controls, will choke off development of future life-saving innovations, costing far more in lost lives over the long run than we'll save in money up-front.

One of the most persistent critics of the industry's profit incentive is Dr. Marcia Angell. In her often-cited 2004 book, *The Truth about the Drug Companies: How They Deceive Us and What to Do about It*, Dr. Angell, a former editor of the prestigious *New England Journal of Medicine*, declared that we should curb "commercial imperatives" by trimming drug patents, narrowing their scope, and sharply curtailing Big Pharma's ability to market new medicines to patients and doctors, as well as its ability to fund clinical research. She also suggested that opening the industry's accounts to the public – as former secretary of state Clinton and Senator Bernie Sanders have called for – would ensure drug prices that are "reasonable" and "as uniform as possible for all purchasers."

Drug companies, Angell believes, should have narrow-but-predictable profit margins. She envisions a world in which drug companies, though heavily regulated and subject to caps on their profits, would be willing to continue supplying vital drugs "as a social service – and a thank-you to the public that subsidizes them so handsomely."

That's not real-world thinking. If it were so cheap and easy to invent effective medicines, India (which traditionally has offered very little in the way of drug patents) would be the drug-producing powerhouse instead of the United States. (And Dr. Angell's "thank you" recommendations for the drug companies should almost certainly be proposed in the opposite direction, to the life-saving innovators.)

When it comes to new medicines, the industry's critics routinely get the economics exactly wrong. While pharmaceutical firms do appear to earn "somewhat higher" profits than the US industrial average, this "could simply reflect a greater cost of capital for the drug industry, commensurate with its riskier investment environment." That riskier investment environment includes the fact that only about 11 percent of all medicines that enter into human trials will ever become FDA approved.

Even during the most costly period of the FDA approval process (phase III clinical trials), the odds of success can be little more predictable than a coin flip. By the time its new type of cholesterol-lowering medicine failed to outperform Lipitor in a head-to-head trial of fifteen thousand patients, Pfizer was out $800 million.

These extremely long and uncertain development timelines are responsible for much of the high cost of drug development. Modernizing drug-trial protocols (which we'll discuss later) would sharply reduce drug-development costs, advance the development of precision medicines, and allow more drugs to reach patients sooner. If a drug company were to face the loss of hundreds of millions of dollars chasing better treatments but couldn't recoup those losses in the form of premium profits on its relatively few successful drugs, its investors would rapidly send their money elsewhere (such as commercial real estate or software).

Drug-development costs have been rising sharply for decades. A 2011 study in the journal *Nature* examined the previous fifty years and found that productivity in the industry declined by 50 percent in each nine-year period looked at, per every $1 billion spent. In significant part, this is due to the increasing cost and time required to collect the safety-and-efficacy information required for FDA approval and, more and more in the current market, to generate the necessary proof that a new drug performs at least as well as other current options.

In 2011, Michael Rawlins, then head of the UK's National Institute for Health and Care Excellence and a frequent critic of industry pricing, noted that the regulatory requirements in both the United States and United Kingdom "[had] increased hugely." In the 1990s, the median number of patients exposed to a new drug in clinical trials was about 1,500; by 2011, that number had grown to 12,000. "It is a huge increase with not much gain, not much benefit from these increased numbers," Rawlins noted. "And of course, it puts up the cost of drug development hugely." He went on to estimate that clinical trials accounted for well over 50 percent of the cost of new drugs.

There is, however, one inexorable channel for making expensive drugs cheap: the expiration of their patents.

* * *

Innovation Today, Generics Tomorrow: A Grand Bargain

If we want the supply of innovative drugs to keep expanding, and eventually to drop in cost, we need to understand the fundamental economics of medical innovation – while also finding ways to close the gap between short-term costs and long-term benefits.

America's remarkably innovative medicine industry benefits from a grand bargain that balances strong incentives to innovate up-front against robust competition – in the form of generic drugs – later. Drug makers have monopolies on patented drugs – lasting from the time the patents take effect to the time they expire and generic competition starts – that run for about ten to eleven years following FDA approval. Americans have access to some of the least expensive generic medicines in the world, and the generic pharmaceutical industry asserts that it has saved US purchasers $1 trillion over the last decade.

In the 1990s, when the first generation of highly effective HIV cocktails was launched, there were concerns that those drugs would be unaffordable for society. Today, the picture looks very different, because the "grand bargain" has worked reasonably well.

The chief strategy officer for GlaxoSmithKline, one of the leading makers of anti-HIV drugs, suggested that his company might not be in the business in another ten years. Current treatments in the industry are so safe and effective, David Redfern mused, that GSK's HIV/AIDS unit, its most profitable unit today, "may no longer have a purpose" once those patents expire. Redfern observed that "the industry has done a fantastic job of taking the fear of the late '80s, and the death sentence, and taking that to one tablet a day." Short of a one-shot cure, there's not much innovation left to be done.

Redfern's right. There are a growing number of generic HIV drugs today, and even the newest brand-name ones will eventually become inexpensive generics.

This is all thanks to a 1980s-era law known as the Hatch-Waxman Act, which struck a Goldilocks-esque bargain between strong initial drug patents (which give investors confidence that they can sink large sums of money into drug development today and recoup their costs and profits a decade later) and cheap generic competition after the patents expire.

Under the act, the creators of brand-name drugs are allowed to recoup some of the time spent navigating FDA-required clinical trials, which can take years. Patents ensure that generic manufacturers can't immediately copy successful drugs and profit off the innovators' work and investment.

But after the patents expire, generic companies are

able to piggyback on the data that the branded companies used to get FDA approval in the first place. Before Hatch-Waxman, manufacturers of generics had to conduct their own clinical trials, just as manufacturers of branded drugs always have. That expensive demand limited generic competition. With Hatch-Waxman, generics can be priced at a fraction of the cost of branded drugs, because they don't face the same high development costs.

With the act, Congress struck a great balance that has endured, with some tweaks, for the last thirty-two years. No law is perfect, but this is probably as close as one could come given existing technology and regulations.

While Hatch-Waxman created the conditions for low-cost generic drugs to thrive, after a decade-long "waiting period" before branded drugs' patents expire, it also created a powerful incentive for brand-name manufacturers to sink billions into the search for new medicines – because they know every billion-dollar blockbuster drug comes with its own sell-by date, and a massive loss of revenue.

America: The World's Indispensable Innovator

Some argue that adopting the profit or price controls that are common in Europe, the UK, and Canada wouldn't curtail innovation. Why are the same drugs that are sold in those countries so much more expensive when purchased in the United States?

With the United States supplying nearly half of the pharmaceutical industry's global revenues, smaller countries can afford to free ride on US investment without the number of innovations reaching their patients obviously

If we want the supply of innovative drugs to keep expanding, and eventually to drop in cost, we need to understand the fundamental economics of medical innovation.

getting reduced. Companies that sell in foreign markets need only generate revenues that help cover operating and manufacturing costs but not R & D costs.

Just like Europeans don't have to spend a lot on defense because they benefit from America's much-greater investment in defense capabilities, their leaders don't have to worry about investing in innovation: American consumers are already underwriting enough drug R & D for the whole world. (If, however, our wealthy competitors abroad were to foot more of the bill, there would be more innovation for everyone.)

By the time the first new pill is approved for sale in the United States, or anywhere else, the drug's development costs are already "sunk." This gives drug companies a powerful incentive to sell to secondary markets – even at much-narrower margins than in America – to help recoup their operating costs and, of course, to earn some measure of profit.

Americans' willingness to pay premium pricing sustains drug innovation that benefits the entire world. Another example of premium pricing's benefits is in the airline industry. Airlines sell tickets at prices determined by consumers' willingness to pay. This maximizes their profits and covers all their fixed costs and, as a result, allows them to charge the lowest-possible average price to those who fly in the back of the plane or board last. By charging high prices to a relatively small cohort of fliers who occupy expensive seats at the front of the aircraft, and much lower prices to those seated in the back, the airline stays in business. American Airlines says 25 percent of its fliers account for 70 percent of its revenue.

If the United States were to follow Europe's example on profit and price controls, the number of medicines reaching future patients would plummet because investors wouldn't have an incentive to underwrite the FDA's lengthy drug-development process.

Countries that control pricing directly (or indirectly, by weakening patents – another way of making inexpensive drugs available faster) do suffer some immediate ill effects: new drugs are launched later in these places, keeping patients waiting for them (sometimes too long to be helped by them).

Consider India, which has very weak patent protection for new medicines. India's large generic drug industry is thus able to launch generic versions of branded drugs quickly – just twelve months, on average, after they are introduced into the country.

Drug makers compensate by waiting years longer to introduce new medicines into India, meaning that patients have to wait an average of five years before as many as half of newly launched drugs become available.

Even Germany, a wealthy European country and the EU's single-largest pharmaceutical market, sees delays. From 2000–10, more than 80 percent of newly launched medicines reached US patients within one year, compared to about 60 percent in Germany.

For cancer medicines, in 2014 there were forty-two new drugs launched in the United States, compared to thirty in Germany. In Italy, patients wait an average of fourteen months for cancer drugs after approval by the EMA, Europe's counterpart to the FDA. For Spain, that wait is nearly sixteen months. A recent report revealed that the UK, where the National Institute for Clinical Excellence caps drug prices and constrains market access, "still ha[s] some of the lowest uptake of new cancer medicines compared with the five largest European economies." The survival rates for UK cancer patient lag well behind other advanced Western European countries. With cancer drugs, a delay of months can translate into someone's death sentence.

If we want life-saving medicines to arrive on our markets – and consequently to much-poorer countries abroad – at the fastest-possible speed, premium pricing in the United States is the rocket fuel that powers the process. It's what funds the expensive up-front investments, long development timelines, and eventual rapid rollout (post–FDA approval) of modern medicines. After all, the first-class airfares, and not the revenue from the coach, are what keep the planes in the air.

America excels in a number of high-tech fields, but when it comes to pharmaceuticals, the United States is far and away the unquestioned global leader. Because of our commitment to innovation and nimble venture-capital markets (a vital source of funding for start-up biotech companies), pharmaceutical companies and the world's best researchers flock to our shores to start biotech companies and work in hubs from Boston to San Francisco.

The benefits flow in the opposite direction, too: Pharmaceutical innovation is also essential to the health of the US economy. US-based drug and biotech companies generate high-paying jobs, pay billions in local and federal tax revenues, and invest in high-tech manufacturing facilities in the country that policy makers wish there were more of.

Furthermore, the benefits from improved health care dwarf even those large direct economic benefits. Economists at the University of Chicago have estimated that gains in personal health just since 1970 have "added $3.2 trillion per year to national wealth." Another study, conducted by our employer, the Manhattan Institute, found that approving a single generation of FDA-approved medicines just a year faster would generate $4 trillion in value for patients as a result of living longer lives.

Calls from our 2016 presidential candidates to regulate cutting-edge drug companies in the same way as we regulate local electric utilities (hardly bastions of innovation) come at a time when better treatments are desperately needed for crippling chronic diseases such as Alzheimer's, diabetes, cancer, and Parkinson's. Without better treatments and cures, these diseases will cost America millions of lives and trillions of dollars in the decades to come.

Treating and caring for patients with Alzheimer's and other forms of dementia cost America $236 billion dollars in 2016 alone, and Medicare picked up $160 billion of those expenses. By 2050, the cost is expected to rise to $1 trillion annually, according to the Alzheimer's Association. And, as we noted earlier, 86 percent of all US health care costs – more than $2 trillion in 2016 – are attributable to chronic diseases. Our best hope for managing, and even reducing, those staggering costs is through innovative medicines and diagnostics.

One particularly promising approach to tackling chronic diseases on the horizon is gene therapy, which allows researchers to snip out faulty versions of genes or replace missing ones with functioning versions. Some versions of these therapies that are close to approval address high-cost ailments such as sickle cell disease, beta-thalassemia, and severe combined immune deficiency (SCID), which can cost hundreds of thousands, or even millions of dollars, to treat annually. The initial pricing of these therapies will reflect both their value and the need to recoup the investments in decades' worth of pioneering trials. As Stuart Orkin and Phillip Reilly wrote:

> *In considering the potential value of gene therapy, it is useful to reflect on the cost of current management of human genetic disorders. Although each disorder affects fewer than 100,000 individuals in the United States, in aggregate they represent an enormous cost to the health care system. For instance, treatment of the >70,000 patients with sickle cell disease (SCD) in the United States exceeds $1 billion per year. These estimates do not take into account lost opportunities from days out of work and the drain on families.*

Prices for gene therapy will undoubtedly appear high, at least in the short term. But payers don't blink at paying for other types of services whose costs accrue over years and decades. Society hasn't balked at the high cost of organ transplants, bone marrow transplantation for blood cancer, or the $42 billion spent annually on dialysis for the seventy thousand or more Americans with end-stage renal disease.

A one-shot cure effected through gene therapy might cost hundreds of thousands of dollars per patient up-front. But over the long term (assuming there is no need for additional therapy and a significantly improved quality and length of life), these drugs will be eminently cost effective, if not cost reducing.

Important lessons can be gleaned from how we conquered HIV/AIDS. Today, drugs make up about 50 percent of the costs of HIV treatment. And their rapid uptake starting in the 1990s, when the first effective combination treatments for HIV/AIDS were launched, has reduced mortality rates by 85 percent. They also turned out to be a bargain from a bottom-line perspective. Truven, a health-analytics firm, estimated that from 1996 to 2010 medicines added about $600 billion in economic value (even after accounting for treatment costs) in the United States by allowing infected patients to work and live longer.

Most of the cost of illness is generated by people being sick – not the medicines used to treat their sicknesses (which, at most, account for 15–20 percent of total US health care spending). Some of those costs are highly visible – like admissions to hospitals and nursing homes – but many of the costs are invisible to payers or off budget entirely, including productivity losses from employees too sick to work; family members who stay home to care for loved ones; or declines in quality of life due to chronic anxiety, pain, or depression. Medicines have been shown to reduce these costs, or even eliminate them entirely (as vaccines and some highly effective drugs do).

In fact, the Congressional Budget Office noted for the first time two years ago that new medicines reduced spending on other forms of health care, such as hospitals and physician services. The Alzheimer's Association estimated that a single new treatment that delayed the onset of Alzheimer's by just five years would save the government health care programs, Medicare and Medicaid, about $200 billion annually by 2050.

Recognizing the full economic burden of disease means acknowledging that the price-control solutions proposed by industry skeptics to curtail costs can't and won't work. Aging isn't optional – nor, for the most part, is getting sick. At some point in all of our lives, we will become patients.

Cancer drug prices are just one area in which a more complete perspective is badly needed. The total share of health spending on cancer in the United States – that is, for

If the United States were to follow Europe's example on profit and price controls, the number of medicines reaching future patients would plummet.

all care, not just for the drugs – has remained constant, at 5 percent, for decades. New cancer drugs were responsible for roughly 1 percent of total health spending, or $42.4 billion, in 2014, according to IMS Health. Researchers at the University of Chicago also estimated that a 1 percent decline in cancer mortality would be worth about $500 billion annually – while a true cure would be worth trillions.

The costs of cancer to the US economy, patients, families, and caregivers are far higher. A 2008 study in the *Journal of the National Cancer Institute* estimated that the total value of lives lost due to cancer deaths in the United States in the year 2000 exceeded $900 billion, and projected the value to rise to $1.47 trillion by 2020. Another estimate pegged the annual productivity losses at around $300 billion.

Cancer drug prices and spending won't keep going up indefinitely. Spending on new drugs that treat cancer at its molecular roots – along with more effective and inexpensive prevention and detection tools that will certainly be developed in the next decade or so – will inevitably help defray the high costs of late-stage cancer treatment by allowing more patients to be put into remission at progressively earlier stages of the disease. This will reduce the need for following up with chemo, radiation, and diagnostic scans. Later, the new drugs will become much-less-expensive generics, and will save even-more lives because time will have taught us how to use them more effectively.

Other diseases will also benefit from market-driven competition. As the rewards of cancer innovation have increased, the number of anticancer compounds in development – well over eight hundred at last count, or 30 percent of all medicines in early-stage testing – has also increased. Many of these drugs are chasing the same molecular targets, and will have to compete head to head, including on price, to get onto payers' preferred formularies.

A special mention should be reserved for the economics of vaccines, which have undoubtedly saved and extended more lives than any other medical innovation in human history. In a tribute to the prolific vaccine innovator Maurice Hilleman, a scientist who worked for decades at the drug maker Merck, the *New York Times* observed that:

> *We live in an epidemiological bubble and are for the most part blissfully unaware of it. Diseases that were routine hazards of childhood for many Americans living today now seem like ancient history. And while every mother could once identify measles in a heartbeat, now even the best hospitals have to call in their eldest staff members to ask: "Is this what we think it is?"*

In 2014, the US Centers for Disease Control estimated that vaccinations would prevent more than twenty-one million hospitalizations and 732,000 deaths among children born in the preceding twenty years.

Newer vaccines such as Gardasil, which protects against the strains of the HPV virus that can most commonly cause cervical cancer, continue to save lives and reduce costs. Researchers estimated that the latest formulation of Gardasil, which is even more effective at reducing the onset of and deaths from cervical cancer (thwarting about 80 percent of cancer-causing viral strains, compared to 66 percent in an earlier formulation), would reduce US health care spending by $2.7 billion over the next thirty-five years.

The science changes but the economics do not. As one of the authors wrote in *The Cure and the Code*:

> *According to estimates made in 1994, every dollar spent on polio vaccine saved about five times as much in . . . [costs that would have been incurred treating or caring for polio victims]. The measles immunization payoff was thirteen to one. In 2001, every dollar spent on immunization with five other widely administered vaccines was saving an estimated $6 in direct medical costs and another $12 in costs of missed work, disability, and death.*

Chapter 4 · Customized Cures, with an Assist from Silicon Valley

When it comes to medicines, one size rarely fits all. While traditional vaccines and some medicines are broadly effective in large populations, better treatments (and lower total health costs) for many serious chronic illnesses – like cancer – will have to be tailored to the biology of the individual patient, an approach called "precision medicine."

To unleash precision medicine, we ought to be looking west for help, to Silicon Valley – and not back east to Washington. A glance at the overall US economy should tell us everything we need to know about what happens when the government dominates the commanding heights of any industry. The tech industry's network of "permissionless innovation" flourishes because its companies don't have to navigate dense webs of federal regulations before launching new products, or wait for government paymasters to tell them what they can charge.

New generations of consumer products offer superior performance at the same or even-lower prices than in the past, adjusted for quality. Just check the smartphone in your pocket, or the computer on your desk: Many consumer electronics are priced the same as the previous year's models, but are more powerful and can do more things (like instantly translating foreign languages).

Because the tech industry's products and services keep it in constant connection with other companies and consumers, it is an industry defined by rapid-cycle innovation. These "digital feedback" loops allow services and products to be tailored and tweaked quickly. That's not true for drugs and medical devices, which have to undergo years – sometimes many years – of expensive, tightly controlled testing required by the US Food and Drug Administration before they can be administered to a single patient outside of clinical trials. There is very little in the way of rapid or real-time feedback loops in the industry – even though the technology for it is available today.

FDA regulators usually want to see a clear one-to-one match between a drug being tested and a positive effect on a group of patients chosen randomly – and, ideally, they want to compare the drug's effect against a placebo. This approach requires lots of patients, time, and risky capital investment (most drugs that are tested fail).

But are all these drugs really failing, or is it the FDA's drug-testing protocol that's failing?

These trial designs were first used in the 1930s, and are built on the assumption that patients with similar clinical symptoms are suffering from the same disease. But that's an assumption that has been disproven by modern science over the past few decades – especially after the deciphering of the human genome in 2000.

New diagnostic tools tell us that, at the molecular level, many seemingly common disorders – so defined by their apparent clinical symptoms – are in fact clusters of biochemically different diseases (breast cancer, for instance, is a combination of at least nine different diseases). But traditional symptom-based definitions of singular diseases are still used to frame most FDA-approved clinical trials, leading to the testing of one drug at a time in patients that are assumed to have the same condition.

Precision medicine (with a digital assist) is the intelligent alternative to this fumbling, and it can be made available to all physicians. It hinges on two deeply intertwined strategies. First, drug designers must be able to precisely target disease-propelling molecular factors ("biomarkers') and pathways. They're getting better at that every year. Second, doctors need to be able to identify, through reliable diagnostic tests, the patients in whom those factors or pathways are present – enabling them to rapidly match a targeted drug with the correct patient profile. From here, completing the feedback loop, doctors and researchers need to be able to follow what happens to patients and adjust the use of medications accordingly.

Left to expert physicians with access to large patient databases that allow them to share reliable information quickly, this feedback strategy can produce a rapid-learning health system that improves care based on what we learn from every patient's response to treatment.

Tragically, many drugs that might be effective for subsets of patients will be tossed into the dustbin just because FDA trials aren't sophisticated enough to allow on-the-fly

Researchers at the University of Chicago estimated that a 1 percent decline in cancer mortality would be worth about $500 billion annually—while a true cure would be worth trillions.

development of the science that will match them with the right patients. Other drugs will be discarded because a small minority of patients will suffer serious side effects – but they will be side effects that don't affect the vast majority of people, whose biochemistry probably differs. (Whether a drug is deemed "safe" can depend on genetic variations that influence such factors as how it is metabolized in an individual patient's liver or how it interacts with the other organ systems, from the heart to the brain.)

FDA regulations not only constrain drug development, delaying access for very sick people and inflating development costs that get passed on to patients, but they can even block drug companies' relay of clinically relevant information about their products. When information doesn't flow effectively, doctors and patients are often left fumbling in the dark for life-saving or life-improving options.

We need to expand our mindset from simply "developing a drug" to "developing the patients." Both matter, of course, but the complex biochemical details that provide invaluable feedback to drug designers all reside inside the patients themselves.

Further complicating this goal is the fact that some diseases (cancers, most notably) mutate rapidly and quickly learn to evade drugs prescribed to treat them. Late-stage cancers mutate so fast that they can rarely be defeated by a single drug. A cocktail, known as "combination therapy" treatment, is required instead.

Mapping these intricate molecular pathways is the great medical challenge of our time. Fortunately, patients and physicians have powerful allies in the tech industry, where companies are tremendously skilled at analyzing large, complex data.

Amazon and Google are already racing to build the largest medical databases of patient-contributed genetic information. Google is aiming to provide the best "analytic tools [that] can fish out genetic gold – a drug target, say, or a DNA variant that strongly predicts disease risk – from a sea of data." Academic and pharmaceutical research projects are currently information services' biggest customers, but Google expects them to be overtaken by clinical applications in the next decade, with doctors using the services regularly "to understand how a patient's genetic profile affects his risk of various diseases or his likely response to medication."

As the National Research Council (NRC) declared in a 2011 report, precision medicine requires a "new taxonomy of disease." Doctors and patients are already helping to build this taxonomy from the bottom up by collecting molecular data and monitoring patient outcomes whenever they prescribe drugs. As they do this, they expose the fundamental and costly shortcomings underpinning too many of the FDA's symptom-driven protocols.

In one off-label trial initiated by oncologists, for example, a kidney cancer drug failed to help over 90 percent of the bladder cancer patients to whom it was prescribed. But it did wipe out the cancer in one seventy-three-year-old patient. A genetic analysis of her entire tumor revealed a rare mutation that made her cancer uniquely responsive to the drug. Similar mutations were found in about 8 percent of patients, and the presence of the mutation correlated well with the cancer's sensitivity to the drug.

In 2013, the National Cancer Institute (NCI) followed up with an announcement of a new "Exceptional Responders Initiative." In June 2014, the NCI started soliciting additional reports about such patients from researchers and doctors nationwide. As of March 2015, more than seventy cases had been provisionally accepted for further analysis, with hundreds more anticipated.

When the distinguishing molecules of exceptional responders align with what the drug was designed to target, these findings could well lead to the resurrection of abandoned drugs that might have helped many patients over the last decade.

Adaptive Trials Enable a Learning Feedback Loop

The long delays in matching drugs with the appropriate patients could have been avoided if analyses had been conducted during the original drug-approval trials under what are called "adaptive trial" protocols. Adaptive trials gather, track, and analyze patient responses to the drug being tested "on the fly" to identify biomarkers that cause certain patients to respond differently to the same treatment regimens.

Adaptive trials can also search for, and find, safety biomarkers by analyzing the patients who suffer side effects. By adding the necessary information to their labels, drugs that wouldn't otherwise be approved could be made available, so that they could reach the patients who would benefit from them.

Just like the digital feedback loop that exists in the world of tech, as the trials progress, adaptive trial protocols evolve. As a result, the collective understanding of the molecular science affecting an individual patient, or patient cohort, improves. The process can continue after the drug is approved, and will keep improving as long as physicians and doctors continue using the drug.

That's the future of medicine – a world of learn-as-you-go medicine driven by customized cures, delivered to the right patient at the right time, at a fraction of the cost required today. But getting there will require commitment and long-term vision.

Innovation is a far-more-effective means of lowering drug costs than government control. That's why we need to make it less risky, less expensive, and less time consuming for researchers and companies to bring new medicines to patients.

If information in the pharmaceutical industry were flowing freely, as it does in the industries that have embraced information technology, continuous data collection, and cloud-based computing, pharmaceutical companies could show how their drugs perform in the real world, on real patients. Then drugs could compete against one another based on outcomes, not just on price. This is a strategy that should apply across the health care sector.

Drug companies are already willing to, and should, take on more of the risk of whether a drug performs as advertised or not. The problem is that most electronic medical records aren't tracking outcomes. If they did, patients' share of the drug cost would decrease because insurers would be able to trust that the drug would deliver outcomes, and perhaps keeping patients healthier longer would save insurers money in the long run.

The good news is that we're already headed in this

direction. By 2018, Medicare plans to make half of its payments to doctors and hospitals based on quality and outcomes, such as the frequency of hospital-acquired infections and hospital readmission within thirty days of a procedure. Since Medicare is the single-largest insurer in the United States, covering all Americans over the age of sixty-five, private insurers are already following its lead – and in many cases getting ahead of it.

Think of it like buying a car. Today, car companies such as Toyota and Ford guarantee that there won't be any major defects in their vehicles' engines or transmissions for six years or sixty thousand miles, and sometimes even longer. If there are problems, they repair the parts for free. And major online rating systems – like Edmunds, J. D. Power, and Kelley Blue Book – help consumers seek out the most reliable brands and models, creating even-greater incentives for manufacturers to design and sell better and safer cars.

Geisinger Health System, in Pennsylvania, does something similar: It guarantees the quality of its heart surgeries. If patients have any complications within ninety days, their insurers aren't charged for any follow-up treatment. Geisinger even refunds part or all of a patient's copays for spinal or bariatric surgery if they are dissatisfied with the quality of their care.

Dr. David Feinberg, the CEO of Geisinger, put it this way:

When you go into a Starbucks and you don't like the coffee, I've never heard a barista say, "No, we made it the right way, you have to drink it . . . ." They just take care of you. This is about patient care, people taking care of people. We want to get it right every time with every patient.

Getting it right every time with every patient should be the aim of the entire health care system. Reimbursement contracts tied to outcomes can allow insurers, drug companies, hospitals, and doctors to stand behind that goal. Online databases collecting information on patient outcomes for common conditions across insurers and providers will encourage even-more competition based on price and quality.

Health systems like Geisinger are the exception, and they shouldn't be. Hospitals and insurers don't make it easy to access information on their outcomes and performance. If you've ever shopped for health insurance, you have probably made your decision based on premiums or whether your personal doctor is in network. Wouldn't it be desirable to know how good their networks are? Or how low your local hospital's infection rate is when you need a surgery? Hospitals advertise heavily, but critical information like this is still too hard to find.

The government should encourage market competition by making it easier for consumers shopping on insurance exchanges to find information on providers' quality and safety. The government should also open databases to commercial researchers and entrepreneurs who can mine the data to determine how specific types of patients – matched for age and health status – fare when they are treated for common conditions. Along the way, companies will undoubtedly develop new platforms and business models that help patients find the care they need – like an Angie's List for medical treatments and services.

Some of these rating systems already exist: Healthgrades, the Leapfrog safety score, and Yelp currently allow patients and consumers to access quality and safety data for doctors and hospitals or to rate their experiences with them. The key is simply making these tools easier to find when consumers need to make critical decisions – like what kind of insurance to buy. Patients will also benefit as prices come down and quality rises as a result of transparency and competition.

Congress should also allow for long-term health insurance contracts, and allow insurers to offer discounts for those contracts. If patients opted to leave the contract early, they should face a financial penalty. (If they left because insurers reneged on promises to offer covered services and treatments, the penalty could be waived.) For users of Obama's health insurance exchanges, states should also offer cost calculators that allow patients to see what their out-of-pocket costs for their medicines

To unleash precision medicine, we ought to be looking west for help, to Silicon Valley – and not back east to Washington.

would be. This would give everyone an incentive to focus on patients' long-term health.

Building pay-for-performance contracts for medicine will be more complicated than it is for surgeries because patient compliance plays a bigger role when it comes to taking prescriptions. If a drug designed to lower a diabetic's insulin doesn't work, is it because the drug was ineffective, or because the patient didn't take it as directed by the doctor, or because he or she didn't eat right? If a patient is taking multiple drugs, which one is the cause of a serious side effect?

Patients will have to take more responsibility for their own care, simply because they're the ones best positioned to do so. Doctors and nurses can help, but we don't want to tie them up badgering their patients (patients don't want that either). For people with serious chronic illnesses like diabetes or hypertension, finding an effective medicine and taking it consistently can mean the difference between living a long, healthy life and suffering disabling or even potentially fatal complications from a poorly controlled disease.

One solution is to make patient monitoring as easy and seamless as possible, and to reward patients for doing the right thing. From the sensors made by Fitbit to the new pacemakers that transmit data wirelessly to your doctor, many new innovations are already helping people with serious chronic conditions live healthier lives.

These developments will also make it much easier for insurers and drug companies to track the effects of medicines, and the costs of such sensors (along with their size) will only continue to shrink. Additionally, these and other diagnostic tools will give patients greater confidence that their medicines are actually worth the price.

Inexpensive genetic tests will help, too. Pharmacogenomics is the science of understanding the role of genetics in how your body processes commonly used drugs, including those for depression, HIV, blood clots, chronic pain, and cancer. An individual's genetic variation can mean the difference between a drug working and him or her suffering from a serious side effect. An inexpensive genetic test can help your doctor personalize your medicines, taking into account diet, exercise, and aging.

When patients take the right medicines responsibly, insurers should waive copays for drugs (both branded and generic) that effectively control chronic illnesses. This is paying pennies for dollars of downstream savings. Not taking medicines for chronic illnesses correctly and consistently may cost the United States $289 billion annually, and contribute to 125,000 unnecessary deaths.

Asking patients to consider which medicine delivers the most benefits for the best price will help keep drug costs in check. Ninety percent of all drugs patients pick up at the pharmacy are generics, often costing $10 or less. Low (or zero-dollar) copayments encourage patients to try the cheaper alternative first to see if it works well. Sometimes we can't ask patients to try a cheaper drug first because their immediate health or lives are at stake. But, in many cases, patient access to effective competing alternatives can help keep costs down – even when those medicines are still patent protected.

Most of our health care problems stem from too-little competition and patient choice, too-much centralized decision making, and a regulatory system that makes innovation stunningly expensive and time consuming. The government needs to strip away the bureaucracy and outdated FDA regulations that make it more difficult for patients and their physicians to unlock the world of precision medicine. Better health at a lower cost is the ultimate promise of precision medicine.

Drug prices are part of an important feedback loop that involves tech-savvy physicians using advanced diagnostics to connect the right patient with the right drug at the right time. The government tries to help patients by suppressing drug prices, but that actually distorts the information provided to investors and developers, and disincentivizes them. When information about price and quality is allowed to flow freely, markets are very good at sorting out the most effective options.

The government needs to lower regulatory barriers to entry so that new competitors can offer patients more options at lower prices. For a while, Gilead made the only hep-C drug on the market, but it had to reduce its price by 50 percent once there were multiple competing alternatives.

This is the role of the health care learning system. Only once a drug is actually used by patients, and their physicians can exchange feedback in real time, do we gain the knowledge to use those medicines most effectively. Physicians often learn better over time how to use medicines and combine them with other approaches (including surgery or lifestyle changes), and apply them in select groups of patients who are more likely to do well. The advance of medicine is an iterative process in which patients and physicians play immensely important, interdependent roles.

This real-world, patient-centered learning is only possible with the big-data analytics provided by Silicon Valley (now embodied in dozens of tech clusters and thousands of companies throughout the United States), and the new payment and contracting strategies being worked out between drug companies, insurers, and providers.

It's time for a twenty-first-century regulatory reboot that accelerates the adoption of customized cures, drives competition across the entire health care system, and better rewards innovators who deliver medical breakthroughs.

But this can happen only if government loosens its grip. Regulations governing drug development and how we pay for medicines often predate the human genome project (2000), the Internet (1994), and the war on cancer (1971).

For instance, federal law still essentially requires Medicaid to cover any medically necessary, FDA-approved drug for all of its sixty million low-income enrollees across fifty state programs. In return for offering all these different drugs to Medicaid recipients, the program enjoys a "best price" guarantee over private payers. But this discourages drug companies from developing pay-for-performance

When information doesn't flow effectively, doctors and patients are often left fumbling in the dark for life-saving or life-improving options.

contracts with private payers, because they will then have to worry about potentially rebating Medicaid's fifty different state programs – a huge segment of the market. If a drug doesn't work as stipulated by a contract and the drug company rebates its entire price to a private payer, it could also have to offer the same 100 percent rebate to millions of Medicaid patients.

When they are working with Medicare, drug companies also worry about triggering fraud penalties by offering these money-back guarantees on their medicines – since the refunds could be viewed as a kickback to encourage providers to use the drug for their Medicare patients. The federal government's Centers for Medicare and Medicaid Services should grant drug companies, insurers, and hospitals the freedom to experiment with risk-sharing contracts that make higher prices contingent on better patient outcomes or reductions in other forms of health care spending.

In return for giving up the "best price" statute, Congress should give states greater latitude to set their own Medicaid drug formularies, as Medicare's private Part D plans do. This would give states more bargaining power but still protect patient access to critical medicines for diseases like cancer. (States would still be able to negotiate their own outcomes-based Medicaid contracts with drug makers.)

Even under today's constrained system, we're seeing more companies in the private sector experiment with outcomes-based contracts. UnitedHealth Group's OptumRx subsidiary, a pharmaceutical benefit manager, or PBM, negotiated a pay-for-performance contract for new hepatitis-C medicines. Humana, another insurer, linked the price of a new cholesterol-lowing drug, Repatha, to its ability to reduce heart attacks. Harvard Pilgrim, a Massachusetts-based insurer, negotiated a price for a diabetes drug, Trulicity, that hinged on its ability to lower diabetics' hemoglobin A1C levels below those achieved by other competing medicines. The goal of these programs isn't to obtain lower drug prices or lower drug spending, per se. As Pilgrim's chief medical officer, Michael Sherman, put it: "What we'd like to see is more people moved from the drugs that aren't higher value to the drugs that are higher value . . . [t]hat reduces hospitalization, which is more important than the rebates. We don't want to go back and say, 'Your drug isn't working.'"

As the federal government gets out of the business of trying to micromanage who gets what price, we'll see contracts like this proliferate. Patients will face fewer barriers to the use of precision medicines if drug prices are linked to their impact on other health care costs downstream, because the feedback loop will give insurers and payers the confidence that drugs are doing what they claim to do. The money the insurer will save on fewer emergency room visits and hospitalizations will allow it to offer lower premiums to its members.

Another essential step in unlocking precision medicine is to continue the reform of the FDA that is currently underway. Drug development should be more predictable, more efficient, and lower costing than it currently is.

Today, the FDA collects real-world information about drug safety. Databases should also be developed to collect data on new treatment strategies that go beyond the uses included on the drug's FDA-approved label. This would help validate new treatment strategies for patients in the eyes of payers and physicians.

If you have ever tried to read the long insert that comes with your medicine, you know how unhelpful it can be. Databases that are constantly updated with real-time information, and curated by the FDA, could instead provide physicians and their patients with a more dynamic, reliable source of information about the medicines they're using. Think of it as a national wiki for the medical community.

Eventually, these databases will be far more valuable

to patients than the inserts in their medication boxes. In fields like cancer and HIV treatment, databases already allow doctors to embrace precision medicine strategies that go well beyond the information on the FDA-approved label or insert.

The process of building these databases can start while medicines are still undergoing clinical trials for FDA approval. The FDA needs to allow the new advanced statistics and clinical trial designs currently applied to cancer to be extended to many more diseases. This would allow doctors to rapidly identify groups of patients who are likely to respond to new medicines based on their genetic data.

Today, drug manufacturers are forbidden by law from communicating clinical or economic data about their products that the FDA hasn't included on the label. That harms patients by preventing their physicians from learning information that might be applicable to their specific situation. That information could also be valuable to insurers and providers when it comes time to negotiate pricing.

Even though we now better understand the molecular basis of many different diseases, the FDA label is still focused on rudimentary clinical signs and symptoms, and insurance coverage often hinges on whether a drug has been approved for a certain condition. This impedes innovations for rare diseases or conditions with few effective treatment options. Using molecularly guided diagnostic tests, physicians can repurpose older medicines for new uses and already are doing so by prescribing the drugs off label. More of this type of innovation would happen if the FDA considered real-world evidence and Congress granted new intellectual property protections for drugs whose patents had expired in order to offset the cost of new clinical trials for them.

Congress should hold the FDA accountable for embracing advanced statistical methods and adaptive clinical trial designs, and for establishing an environment in which truthful, scientific, and economic information can flow freely among physicians, insurers, and drug companies.

Critics may counter that it is unethical to use patients as guinea pigs, but conventional trials already do so – slowly and at enormous cost. Whenever they prescribe medicines off label, doctors are extrapolating from their experience and fine-tuning new potential treatments. The unethical option is clinging to outdated standards when more precise strategies are available.

Studies have also established that patients are much more willing to participate in trials if they are assured of being treated with an actual drug, not a placebo. Using this approach will address the increasingly vocal "right-to-try" demands from patients suffering from serious diseases who desperately want rapid access to any drug that might help.

We already have a paradigm of how this "learn as you go," database-driven prescribing strategy would work: It is how physicians at advanced medical centers are currently beating cancer. If we don't expand this approach beyond cancer, our international competitors will, and as a result, they will lure R & D investment overseas. The head of the EMA noted that the new adaptive trials approach could reduce "by years" the time taken to win approval for a new medicine, and that the agency's "expectation is that companies will reflect this by reducing the price of medicines for the benefit of patients and for the sustainability of our health care systems."

Financial Innovations for Expanding Patient Access to Critical Medicines

That's what Washington can do to help lower the cost of precision medicine for patients. The private sector should also be encouraged to think outside the box. Here are some places to start:

- Employers currently rely on third-party negotiators, in the way of PBMs, to design their formularies and negotiate discounts on drug prices. It's not always clear, however, that employers receive the full benefit of drug company rebates using this system. They can demand more transparency from PBMs, and pay them on a flat-rate basis. Some employers already do this, but more need to.

- Insurers should give patients the benefit of the discounts they negotiate with drug companies when calculating the patient's coinsurance for high-cost specialty medicines.

- Providers, or even drug companies, could offer "medical mortgages" for high-cost curative treatments. This would allow patients to amortize their share of drug costs over much longer periods of time, much as we do today for home loans, college tuition, and new car payments. If the drugs didn't work, or stopped working, a patient's remaining debt could be forgiven.

- Insurers should give physicians an up-front payment to care for patients with complicated diseases who need care coordination, and let the doctor decide what medications might offset the need for hospitalizations, emergency room visits, surgeries, or other medical services, while still delivering the best outcome.

- Instead of just offering medicines a la carte, drug companies could offer an entire suite of their products to providers for a negotiated fee in order to ensure maximum patient and physician access to effective options. The fee could be updated as new treatments come online.

Tech- and software-savvy companies and entrepreneurs will play an increasingly large role in this patient-focused, value-driven revolution. Empatica, a start-up wearable tech company cofounded by MIT professor Rosalind Picard, makes a research-quality wearable device that can monitor children at risk for potentially life-threatening epileptic seizures. Google is working on contact lenses that monitor diabetics' blood sugar. Grail, a spin-off company from Illumina, is working on a blood biopsy that can detect circulating-tumor DNA in asymptomatic individuals – which can allow for a cancer early-warning system that may eventually enable doctors to prescribe drugs to stop the disease in its tracks. Smartphones already have the capability to

One day, each one of us – or our loved ones – will be a patient in need. When that day comes, the cost and quality of the treatments available to us will hinge on the decisions made by policy makers to embrace innovation or to undermine it.

collect health data and send it wirelessly and securely to your doctor's office. All of these tools, and more, will help us use medicines more effectively in the future.

Over time, trusted data sources and diagnostics will accelerate the pace of innovation and reduce spending on wasteful or dangerous treatments.

Between the reality of today's trial-and-error prescribing system and tomorrow's precision medicine that will detect and treat life-threatening ailments before they become debilitating and expensive, much work remains to be done. The Obama administration is spearheading the Precision Medicine Initiative, while also calling for the National Cancer Moonshot. Bipartisan congressional leaders have passed the 21st Century Cures Act, which accelerates the development of contemporary cures and helps reform the FDA – it should reach the president's desk in 2016.

One day, each one of us – or our loved ones – will be a patient in need. When that day comes, the cost and quality of the treatments available to us will hinge on the decisions made by policy makers to embrace innovation or to undermine it.

Our medical future will involve much of the customization and rapid-cycle learning that we see today in the rest of America's high-tech economy – that is, if Washington doesn't throttle it first with misguided price controls.

First American edition published in 2016 by Encounter Books, an activity of Encounter for Culture and Education, Inc., a nonprofit, tax exempt corporation.
Encounter Books website address: www.encounterbooks.com

Manufactured in the United States and printed on acid-free paper. The paper used in this publication meets the minimum requirements of ANSI/NISO Z39.48–1992 (R 1997) (*Permanence of Paper*).

FIRST AMERICAN EDITION

LIBRARY OF CONGRESS CATALOGING-IN-PUBLICATION DATA IS AVAILABLE

Howard, Paul.
Unlocking Precision Medicine / by Paul Howard & Peter Huber.
pages cm. — (Encounter intelligence ; 2)
ISBN 978-1-59403-917-1 (pbk. : alk. paper) —
ISBN 978-1-59403-918-8 (ebook)

10 9 8 7 6 5 4 3 2 1

SERIES DESIGN BY CARL W. SCARBROUGH